Discover New Bern

May it be hoped that what has been preserved may be long retained, and not marred by new and strange ideas, which however suitable to the places that have developed them, would be here merely imitative, and would perhaps destroy those very differences that make this place so interesting. It is not what is new, but what is incongruous, that should be avoided.   –Alice R. H. Smith, 1917

Printed in China

Book and cover design by
Sunbury Design
sunbury@marshmud.net
QuarkXpress; Apple Macintosh.
Galliard with
Adobe Garamond figures.

ISBN 978-1-937921-02-6

1 3 5 7 9 10 8 6 4 2

previous page – The authentic green paint of the ★Cutting-Allen house shutters is based on recent extensive paint research.

this page – "Bears" is the name of Bern, Switzerland; bears are its icon. Bears are also the icon of New Bern; these beasts on the central fire station and the city hall were purchased by order of the Board of Aldermen in 1914 from the S. B. Parker Co., who got them from a firm in New York.

title page – The tallest structure in the historic area is the steeple of Christ Church, 1875. The records are not clear as to whether the gilded copper crown signifies the crown of life or the fact that this was the viceregal chapel in the years before the Revolution. That doesn't matter to the ospreys that sometimes nest there.

Discover New Bern

by Richard Parsons

With interior photographs by
Zach Frailey

Published for the
New Bern Preservation Foundation
by Robbins Hunt

2012

SPONSORS

J. M. Hodges, Jr. in honor of
Cindy Turco

J. M. Hodges, Jr. in honor of
Elizabeth Taylor Hodges

J. Brent, Alecia, and Austin Davis
in memory of
Howard and Harriet Davis

Ann Maude

Paige and Rob Miller in memory
of Dr. and Mrs. William H. Bell

Nancy and Joe Mansfield

Carolina Creations in honor of
Jan and Michael Francoeur

Champ and ET Mitchell in honor
of Joe and Nancy Mansfield

Bill and Nancy Hollows in
memory of Dorothy W. Lindley

Emily and George Henson

BB&T
serving communities since 1872

Dottie Corning in memory of
Jane Millns

Tom and Pat Schaible

Linda Lee Leslie

Historic Riverside
Neighborhood Association

John and Cheryl Young

Coldwell Banker Willis-Smith Co.

Gary and Ashley Baxter Curry
in honor of Mr. and Mrs.
Benjamin Hunt Baxter, Jr.

Paul Switzer in memory of
Patricia D. Switzer

Barbara and Tom Causey
in memory of Otto Herderich

Priscilla Failmezger in honor of
Aaron and Lenora Chauvin

Raymond and Mary Tait

Dr. William L. Hand, Jr.
in memory of
William L. Hand, Jr., D.D.S.

Anne Porter in memory of
Harry W. Porter, Jr.

Twice as Nice

Elizabeth and David Ward

Don and Katie Hodges

Linda Lore in memory of
Richard Lore

Nick and Claire Chauvin in
memory of their dad, Aaron

John L. Griffin in memory of
Elizabeth E. Griffin

James R. Sugg and Jane B. Sugg
in honor of Nelson McDaniel

Buzz and Bette Mead

Pete and Firth Monte in memory
of Robert R. Monte

Genevieve Moeckel
in honor of Bryan Smith

Carolyn and Charles Peterson
in honor of
our children and grandchildren

Jim and Anne Schout

Dr. and Mrs. Andrew D. Mylander
in memory of Chloe and Buster

Penelope Morton Bender
in memory of
J. Wesley and Ethel W. Morton

John Phaup in memory of
Jordan G. Phaup

Lorraine Hale Music Instruction

Dallas and Denise Blackiston
in memory of
Dallas O. Blackiston and
Allen Moreau

Mr. and Mrs. Richard L. Wagner, Sr.
in honor of
Patrick, Matthew, Sophia, Dylan,
and Kaylee

PLAT – The Preservation Legal
Action Trust, Inc.

Dr. John and Maria Cho

Dr. J. Kenneth and Ellen T. Chance
in honor of Kay Phillips Williams

Don and Liane Crawford

Mark and Lynne Harakal in honor
of the New Bern Historical Society

Phillip and Patti Urick and the
Historic Downtown
Residents' Association

Michael and Malinda Breda

Beverly E. Perdue
and Robert W. Eaves

Sandy and Newsom Williams

Mr. and Mrs. Joseph M. Hunt III

The New Bern Woman's Club

Dr. T. Reed and Alice G. Underhill
in memory of
Dr. Dale T. and Jane K. Millns

Mary and Ben Parrish

Warren & Miller Family Dentistry
in memory of
Mr. and Mrs. Julien Knox Warren, Jr.

Tim Thompson in honor of
Billy and Martha Ann Smith

Staff and commissioners of the
City of New Bern
Historic Preservation Commission
in honor of Michael Avery

CENTURY 21 Zaytoun-Raines

*I*N CELEBRATION of the fortieth anniversary of our founding, the Board of Directors of the New Bern Preservation Foundation authorized publishing this commemorative volume entitled *Discover New Bern*. The book highlights some of the splendid historic homes of our community, many of them saved through the efforts of the Foundation.

Established in 1972, the New Bern Preservation Foundation is a tax-exempt charitable non-profit organization whose mission is to preserve historically significant structures and sites in and around New Bern. More than 65 historic residences, mostly in the Historic Downtown District, have been saved by the active work of the Foundation in buying, preserving and reselling them to individuals respectful of their history and significance to this special City.

We do not seek preservation for its own sake, to maintain the status quo, but rather to inspire new activities in keeping with the nature of the community. We encourage development and infill of vacant properties through sharing that sense of history communicated by what has been done.

Preservation is an economic force as well. Many new residents tell us that their first visit to this beautiful city as tourists, or as members of a military family, or in attending a convention, encouraged them to inquire of real estate agents about living in this community. While not all people are willing to reside in an historic home, the open, friendly atmosphere they encounter walking downtown or along the tree-lined streets of the Historic Districts help make their decision to move here.

The current economic vitality of the city in part can be traced to the early work of the Preservation Foundation. Though residing in Greenbrier, Taberna, River Bend, Fairfield Harbour or Carolina Colours, to name a few, each resident takes pride in living within the City of New Bern.

Visit our website (www.newbernpf.org).

Joseph Mansfield, *President*, New Bern Preservation Foundation

New Bern Preservation Foundation Protected Properties are indicated in yellow. Purple indicates other protected properties.

In addition, the NBPF holds covenants on two structures in the Riverside Historic District.

Buildings marked in the text of the book with a ★star are the protected properties shown above.

$\mathcal{P}$ASSING through on the way to summer camp when I was nine years old, I could tell there was something special about New Bern. My baptism into New Bern buildings began the summer I got a driver's license, with a visit to the rather ratty John Wright Stanly house, which at that time housed the public library. Before that special summer was over, I had the rare privilege of meeting "Miss Pearl" and "Mr. Tull" and being shown "Bellair," the John-Hawks-derived brick plantation house, from top to bottom. I also browsed in Bess Guion's antique shop, proudly advertised as being "in the old historic district" and in another antique shop, with its boozy old proprietor, housed in the Joseph Rhem house.

By the early 1980s I was frequently passing through on my way to the sailing fleet "down in the county." I grieved over the ★Thomas Sparrow house standing gaunt, alone, and obviously destined for demolition. I was the one who suggested that it might be more profitable for the owner to give the house to a preservation non-profit organization than to demolish it. The star in front of the name tells the tale; it has been protected by a covenant donated to the Preservation Foundation in 1982.

About the same time, I began to help Peter Sandbeck with his important book, camping with him on weekends in a slum apartment in the unrestored ★Marshall-Lane house and later in a garret apartment of the Wade-Meadows house. In prowling New Bern with Peter for that book, I saw attics, basements, cisterns, church towers, and all the distinctive and recognizable woodwork that comes together to make "New Bern style."

By 1984, one specific early house kept jumping in my face; I bowed to fate and bought it. In 1999 I gave the Preservation Foundation a covenant on it.

This book is a very abbreviated and personal essay; there is only room for a small part of what I find so wonderful about New Bern. I hope you will enjoy New Bern with me through these photographs. For every photograph in this book, we took another ten that need to be included in future books.

Importantly, these are residences – homes – not museums. They are the real-life scenes of births, and deaths, and wedding nights. I invite you to stroll with me through these pages in no particular order, and stroll as much as you can through our streets, enjoying the pageant of a city which is at the same time very old and vibrant with the present.

–R.P.
Hancock-street, 2012

Much of New Bern's wealth came from shipping and commerce, not plantations. New Bern's personality is still defined by its location on the broad waters of the Neuse and Trent Rivers. The water lies just out of sight in many of these photographs.

The skipjack *Ada Mae*, built at Rose Bay in 1915, is the oldest commercial vessel still active in North Carolina. She lies ready to depart from Persimmons Wharf at the foot of Pollock Street.

10 *above* New Bern is not just old houses; it's furniture and flowers, too. Here are four varieties of New-Bern-grown camellias on a two hundred year old mahogany table. The motto *Plus fait douceur que violence* on the plate works out in English to *Make love, not war*.

below The Baptist Church, 1848, glows in late Autumn sunset.

The Palmer-Tisdale house, *ca.* 1769, *ca.* 1800, *ca.* 1830, (*left*), on its original site, finds a good neighbor in the ★Cutting-Allen house, 1793, *ca.* 1856, moved here in 1980. (*right*)

above Both locals and visitors appreciate a special ministry at Christ Church, the little playground: *All are welcome in this place.* In the background, a window of the Stanly Hall ballroom, *ca.* 1874.

below Mid-19th-century luxury in the passage of the John D. Flanner house, *ca.*1855, on Johnson Street.

above The Smallwood-Howard house, *ca.*1815, on Change Street. The passage features an elliptical arch and a modillion cornice. At the rear is a typical New Bern Federal stair, with square-tapered newel, a "biscuit" at the end of the handrail, rectangular pickets, and wave-shaped brackets on the step ends.

below The double parlors of the John D. Flanner house.

A preservation success story, one of the *ca.* 1859 houses of "Cottage Row," ★814 N. Craven Street, before and after.

above The ★Marshall-Lane house, built in the early 19th century, was remodeled about 1850 by builder Hardy B. Lane as his residence and also
to serve as a striking advertisement of his work, with sawn cornice brackets and a fashionable low-pitched roof.

below The living room is brightened by an entire wall of paintings by
Steve Keene, called the "Assembly-Line Picasso" by *Time* magazine.
Through the doorway can be seen the stair, probably dating from Hardy
B. Lane's remodeling.

above The dining room of the ★Marshall-Lane house displays New Bern Federal-style woodwork from the time of its construction *ca*. 1805-10 for William Marshall

below Locavores delight in the Saturday offerings of the Farmers Market at the foot of Hancock Street.

The Coor-Bishop house was built, believe it or not, between 1767 and 1778. It gained its present-day appearance in 1904, when it was heavily remodeled for wealthy commission merchant Edward K. Bishop.

The 18th century staircase was untouched in the remodeling. The explosively beautiful carved brackets were identified by carving specialist John Bivins as New Bern work.

above The first-floor front room of the *ca.* 1805 Thomas Jerkins house; the oil on artist board of the three-masted schooner *G. J. Cherry* is by Antonio Jacobsen. The present owner's father, Captain John Day, was master and half owner of the *Cherry*; he brought the stool by the fireplace back from one of his voyages to Africa.

below The second-floor front room, which originally stretched across the entire front of the house, has a modest chimneypiece, but the window surrounds, the cornice, and the chair rail are quite elaborate.

The City Hall was built as the Federal Building in 1895-97; the clock tower was added in 1910.

The dials of the clock, with a white bulb at every hour and red bulbs at the ends of the hands, is a familiar nighttime sight both by land and from the river.

Architectural details:

above left in the Palmer-Tisdale-Jones house, 1769, this detail *ca.* 1810.

above right a delicate arch in the Thomas Daniels rental house, *ca.* 1895,
    on Hancock Street.

below New Bern Federal in the ★Coor-Cook house, *ca.* 1815.

top left The elaborate portico of the Eli Smallwood house, *ca.* 1810.

top right The Smallwood-Howard house, *ca.* 1815.

below Bright in autumn sun, glossy magnolias bracket the windows of the Walter and Maggie Burrus house, *ca.* 1890, purchased by U.S. Senator Furnifold McLendel Simmons in 1908.

above The second-floor front room of the Eli Smallwood house, *ca.* 1810. Every door, every window, and the chimneypiece are all embellished with Georgian pediments executed with Federal molding This retardataire mixing is typical of the New Bern Federal style.

below The niches and matching looking glasses in the dining room.

In Cedar Grove Cemetery

Judge Gaston's monument in the extreme Grecian style was designed by A. J. Davis.

Eliza Hughes's urn was created by "R. E. Launitz, N-York." Such extravagance suggests the wealth of antebellum New Bern.

above The ★Thomas McLin house, still on its original site, was built as a cottage *ca.* 1820. Evidently damaged in the great fire of 1922, it was over-built shortly thereafter. It has been neatly rehabilitated.

below Thomas and Eliza McLin sleep in Cedar Grove Cemetery, just a block from where they lived.

Cedar Grove Cemetery was established by Christ-Church Parish in 1799 when the churchyard (New Bern's principal burying place for people of all faiths) was filled with the mass graves of victims of yellow fever. Cedar Grove was known as the Episcopal Cemetery until ceded to the city in 1853; the next year the gateway was built of the local "shell rock."

An inscription on the arch reads,
> *Still hallowed be this spot where lies*
> *Each dear loved one in Earth's embrace.*
> *Our God their treasured dust doth prize.*
> *Man should protect their resting place.*

The porous masonry holds rainwater and drips for weeks after a hard storm. Tradition states that if the weeping arch drips on anyone, that one will be the next to pass through in a coffin.

The train is coming! Almost everyone remembers a panic-filled first encounter with the locomotive on Hancock Street. This has been a common sight in New Bern since 1859.

The Christian Science Church, 1907, (*above*) and
Temple Chester B'nai Sholom, 1908 (*below*)
were both designed by New Bern architect Herbert Woodley Simpson.

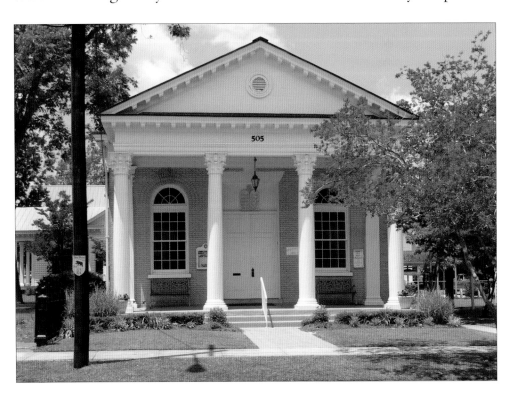

above The date of this house, *ca.*1841-45 suggests it should be classed as Grecian, but the form and massing of ★The Dr. Edward F. Smallwood house are typical New Bern Federal. Just to confuse matters, all the moldings have Grecian profiles. The slightly later front and side piazzas show in an 1863 photograph. The Italianate front piazza replaced a small portico; recent repairs revealed the outline of the earlier roof.

above The Grecian-style Charles Slover house, 1848-1849. The household included Slover, his wife, eight children, and twelve slaves. Both the Rhem and Slover houses were built by the New Bern master builder Hardy B. Lane and his three sons, Frederick, Hardy B. junior, and John.

below The Joseph L. Rhem house (*ca.* 1855) was an architectural first cousin to the Slover house until it was remodeled *ca.* 1913-24.

New Bern's wonderful wedding cake was designed in 1903 by Herbert Woodley Simpson for Maryland lumber baron William B. Blades.

New Bern was North Carolina's wealthiest town from its establishment as the capital in 1765 until the Panic of 1819. The city remained fairly strong until the Unpleasantness of 1861-65.

A distinct New Bern Georgian style flourished during the lifetime of English architect John Hawks (†1790).

A strongly distinctive New Bern Federal style developed in the early 19th century, probably through the influence of William Nichols.

Then nationally-popular Grecian and Italianate styles influenced local architecture until construction mostly halted in the early 1860s.

By the late 19th and early 20th centuries, local architecture, even when designed by hometown architect Simpson, had lost all local influence; landmarks such as the Blades, Mace, and D. M. Parker houses could just as plausibly be in Charleston, San Francisco, or Milwaukee.

30

above The fire station of 1928, with its iconic bear, is being rehabilitated to house the New Bern Fireman's Museum. Behind is the cupola of the 1932 Federal Building, designed by New Bern-born Robert F. Small-wood.

below The *ca.* 1885 Windley Building on Middle Street. The right half originally housed "Jimmie" Moore's saloon and billiards parlor. Today, thanks to preservation, New Bern has a bustling downtown.

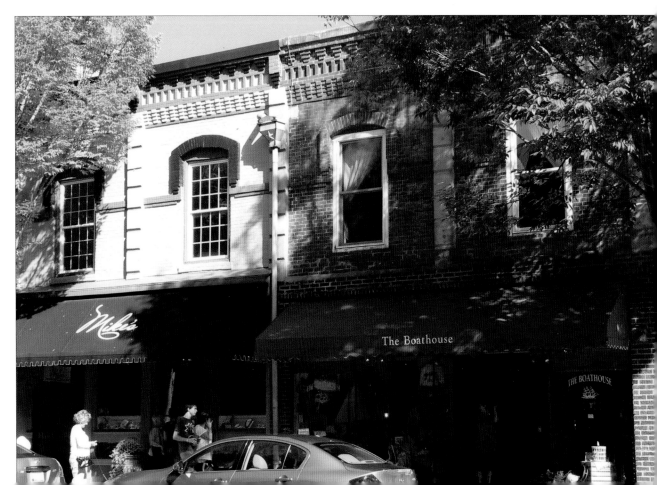

left Carved Roman Ionic capitals grace the unfluted columns of the 1819 Presbyterian Church. Uriah Sandy was the contractor; Martin Stevenson and John Dewey were craftsmen.

above The organ was built by C. B. Fisk of Gloucester, Massachusetts, in 1984.

The Shriners put on a major parade every year. Part of the typical fun, even if it rains, is a brown mule pulling a black hearse and some suits on Segways.

above Sunset over the Trent River and Lawson Creek, seen from the embankment at the foot of Tryon Palace.

below Across the Neuse River, seductive little Duck Creek, with its enigmatic swimming tree, offers harbor for all kinds of small craft.

The Riverside Historic District lies on both sides of National Avenue. Local architect Herbert Woodley Simpson designed this house for William Dunn senior, built in 1913. The stair, seen here from the living room, winds all the way to the attic.

above Stylish details on the John M. Aberly bungalow, *ca.* 1922, National
Avenue, Riverside.

below The Wm. R. Guion house, *ca.* 1894, National Avenue, Riverside.

Four views of the stylish Craftsman bungalow of David M. Parker, *ca.* 1918, on National Avenue in the Riverside Historic District.

According to Sandbeck's *Historic Architecture of New Bern*, the Charles Bates house was built *ca.* 1802-05.

The Attmore-Oliver house began life about 1790 as a story-and-a-half cottage. It was remodeled to this present form about 1834 as a wedding present from Isaac Taylor to his daughter Mary upon her marriage to George Attmore. They gave it to their daughter Hannah Oliver in 1860. The New Bern Historical Society purchased it from the Oliver estate in 1953. The delicate little porch is typical of the retardataire style to be found in New Bern; Federal in form and delicacy, it is finished with the most up-to-date Grecian moulding. The house is open to the public.

The Charles L. Ives house, *ca.* 1895; Colonial Revival piazza and sleeping
porch added in the early 20th century. "Das Merc" the 1959 Mercedes,
and the purple jogging stroller are only two of many exotic vehicles that
live here. "Kitty," the black 1959 Jaguar sedan and the red 1954 XK-120,
frequently seen on the street as well, are only two of a dozen Jags. The
BMWs are just utility vehicles.

above The best bedchamber in the Ives house, with a 19th-century
bedstead believed to have come from Bellair plantation.

below The Ives house library/music room. Gretel the weinerdog nestles
in her basket. The mantel appears to be part of the early-20th-
century remodeling.

New Bern has always had prosperous African-Americans. These two houses were both owned and occupied by prominent free man of color John Carruthers Stanly, reputed natural son of John Wright Stanly. J. C. Stanly was apparently a house carpenter, based on the apprentices he took. He bore the soubriquet "Barber Jack," because he owned a barber shop – operated by two of his slaves – and also to distinguish him from his father. He first lived in the Stanly-Allen house (*above*) from 1807 to 1818, then in the Stanly-Bishop house (b*elow*) until 1831.

above A cluster of "captain's walks" can be seen on Johnson Street. They were really firefighting platforms in the days of wooden roofs.

below At the other end of Johnson Street the tower of St. Cyprian's Church lifts high the cross. St. Cyprian's, designed by local architect Herbert Woodley Simpson, was built 1910-12. After the Great Fire of 1922, the church housed an important relief hospital.

above The Margaret M. Hanff house, *ca.* 1870-80.

above The gentle climate allows the Margaret M. Hanff house piazza to be developed as a tropic sitting room.

below The Hanff front bedroom is a Victorian fantasy designed by the owner's son, Martin Huber Miller of Era Vintage Modern in Houston.

above The façade of the exuberant Ulysses Mace house, 1884, sparkles in the afternoon sun on Broad Street.

below The curving staircase of the Mace house is extensively decorated with stencilling by the owner.

The Florence E. Hanff house, *ca.* 1860-69, on Hancock Street, has a totally unaltered exterior and a totally modern master bathroom where the front parlor used to be.

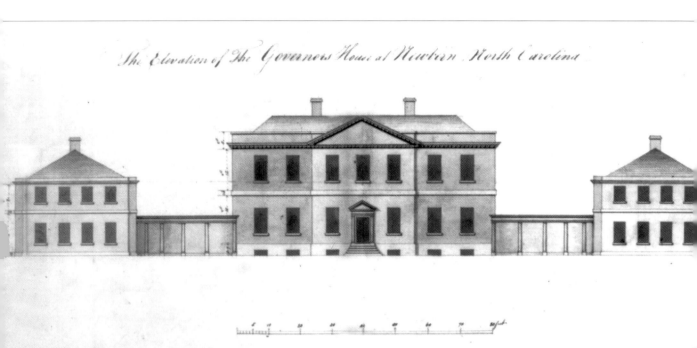

In 1765, Royal Governor William Tryon employed an architect in England, John Hawks, and brought him to New Bern to design and supervise the construction of a "Governor's House" or "Palace;" *palace* at that time had no negative connotations, but was the word describing an official residence of any sort. The edifice they raised was one of the largest and finest pieces of construction in all the Colonies. The Palace was completed in 1770 and superceded as the capitol in 1792. In 1798 it was accidentally burned by a slave woman with a pine-knot torch who was searching the hay stored in the basement for eggs from her hens.

The stable block (the building at the right) survived the fire and the ensuing years; it is a priceless original part of the Palace.

The importance (and magnificence) of the Palace remained legendary in New Bern in succeeding years. The first fund-raising effort for a reconstruction was held in 1929. The discovery of Hawks's original contract drawings in the Public Record Office in London made possible an accurate reconstruction.

In the early 1940s, Maude Moore Latham, native New Bernian, established two trust funds for the reconstruction. In 1945 the State of North Carolina made the first of several appropriations for the project. Construction began in 1950 and was completed in 1959.

Over fifty years later, the reconstructed Palace and its adjacent original structures remain an educational and beautiful part of the New Bern experience. The Palace – its physical presence, collections of decorative arts, politics, and the ups and downs of its finances – dominates the town today just as it must have in the 1770s.

In addition to its kitchen, stable, and other outbuildings, the present-day Tryon Palace, a semi-autonomous state agency, owns a number of other historic houses and maintains extensive gardens. The Governor's House and its offices and gardens, along with other historic structures in the area, are open to the public.

Much of New Bern's charm comes from spots of unexpected beauty amid its gritty reality. Both sides of lower Hancock Street sometime seem like the wrong side of the tracks, but amid the utility poles and railroad high iron, an *Albizia julibrissin* (known locally as Mimosa) bursts with summertime joy alongside the 18th-century Fenner house.

below The ballroom of the 1793 ★Cutting-Allen house was added about 1856 by Allen G. Eubank.

52

above The chimneypiece in the ★Cutting-Allen second floor front room features a Wall-of-Troy fret. Although Wall-of-Troy is not exclusive to New Bern (it can be seen in the great cabin of Nelson's *Victory*, for example), it is the enrichment of choice in New Bern's Georgian buildings.

below Another Wall-of-Troy fret, in the modillion cornice of the Charles Bates house.

above In addition to its larger houses, New Bern is rich in working folks' houses from the early 19th century. The Richard Dowdee house, *ca.* 1828, sits in forlorn isolation across from a convenience store and an abandoned service station on Broad Street.

below Spider Lilies, Hurricane Lilies, *Lycoris radiata*, introduced directly from Japan by New Bernian Captain William Roberts in 1854, appear without warning in early fall in hundreds of yards, in Cedar Grove cemetery, or amid a pile of builder's debris.

above The ★Coor-Cook house, was begun by James Coor for his daughter about 1790, but was not finished until about 1815. The Grecian wing, piazza, and office were added about 1850. Both structures were moved here in 1981 to make room for a jail.

below The library (*ca.* 1850); the juke box is later.

above   The Judge John Donnell (pronounced locally as if followed by Duck) law office, 1816-1819, originally one room with an entry, was moved to Trent Woods in the 1970s and a new house built nearby to compliment it. The lofty barrel-vaulted ceiling of the entry frames an early 20th-century filing cabinet.

below   The office itself is embellished with the original arched bookcases.

On Confederate Memorial Day, 1909, Craven County dedicated the Caswell Branch Bridge. Its restoration in 2007 was a project of the New Bern Preservation Foundation, using funds from the North Carolina Department of Transportation.

This main highway from New Bern to Kinston was unpaved until after 1918, when it was paved with brick, nine feet wide.

A second marble plaque on the bridge parapet states helpfully, 7 MILES TO COURT HOUSE NEW BERN.

above St. John's Lodge Room, on Hancock Street, has elaborate woodwork of 1808 and later painted decorations of 1860.

below The Craven County Court House of 1883. The 1802 courthouse burned just a few months before the Union army captured New Bern in March of 1862. The economic reverses of the Unpleasantness were severe; it was over twenty years before the county got back on its feet enough to build a new court house.

above The Dr. Joseph Latham house, 1928, in the Riverside Historic District. Dr. Latham is remembered for having named St. Cyprian Relief Hospital Dillahunt; in his adulthood, Cyp changed his name to St. Cyprian Relief Hospital Jones.

below Marble sculpture by Horace L. Farlowe (1933-2006).

The Mary Louise Turner house, *ca.*1891 *(left)*. The diminutive Hibbard house, *ca.*1820, *(right)* was moved and enlarged *ca.* 1875-80. It is said to be the birthplace of prominent free Black "Barber Jack" Stanly.

below The staircase of the Hibbard house (or George Bishop rental house,) *ca.*1875, leads to the attic and its original copper bathtub.

opposite page above Nora gnaws her chew on the living room carpet at the Mary Louise Turner house.

opposite page below The Turner house kitchen. The brownies and lime ice water were a delicious unexpected treat, not a photo prop.

above The dutch-roofed ★Mary and Patrick Gordon house, built in His Majesty's loyal Province of North-Carolina in 1771, is likely the oldest largely unaltered house in New Bern; its piazza was added in 1783, just before Mrs. Gordon's death. The large center window was originally the front door.

below This Gordon house paneled overmantel is part of the 1771 finish; the New Bern Federal chimneypiece is a modernization of *ca.* 1815.

above The Georgian staircase in the Gordon house.

below Shell-edged pearlware shards, usually blue like this platter, but sometimes green, are among the most common finds in New Bern archeology (or when digging the garden). In the Gordon "new kitchen" (*ca.* 1892) a plate of chocolate tarts is set out to cool. The "old kitchen" was in the basement, with the wine cellar and laundry.

ACKNOWLEDGMENTS

All dates, house names, and much history are conformed to Peter Sandbeck's scholarly and invaluable *Historic Architecture of New Bern and Craven County,* published by the Tryon Palace Commission in 1988.

A tremendous thank you goes to the homeowners who allowed the camera's invading eye: John and Cheryl Young, George and Emily Henson, Todd Willis and Loyal Oster-lund, Michael and Malinda Breda, Stevens and Betsy Pinkerton, Don and Liane Crawford, Ben and Marion Bunn, Dru Eckberg, Anne Porter, Elizabeth Fuller, Joe and Nancy Mansfield, Julien and Melinda Warren, Lois and Lisa Evans, Mary and Arthur Silver, Fred and Muriel Latham, Bruce Laviolette, Melinda Robinson, Sarah and Mike Afflerbach, Billy and Martha Ann Smith, the Scottish Rite and St. John's Lodge, John and Roberta Delk.

A special thank-you goes to Zach Frailey, the Uprooted Photographer, who made the interior photographs. He has a keen eye, willingness to please, a strong sense of cooperation, and great patience.

Thanks to John B. Green, who read the proof for historical errors. Such errors as remain are the responsibility of the author.

And thanks to Tammy Banks, of Village Graphics, Grantsboro NC, who helped so much during the proof stage of this project.

George waits patiently at the door of "Poor Charlie's,"
a flea market near the foot of Hancock Street,
clearly indicating that this is
The End.